Piano Duets

by
David Carr Glover
and
Louise Garrow

This book is for your first experience in playing duets. It includes familiar tunes as well as attractive originals.

It is correlated with The Piano Student, Level One, of the David Carr Glover PIANO Library.

CONTENTS

© 1970 BELWIN-MILLS PUBLISHING CORP.
All Rights Administered by WARNER BROS. PUBLICATIONS U.S. INC.
All Rights Reserved including Public Performance for Profit

F.D.L. 461

Swing Me Lightly

Secondo

Moderato

Swing Me Lightly

Primo

4

Secondo

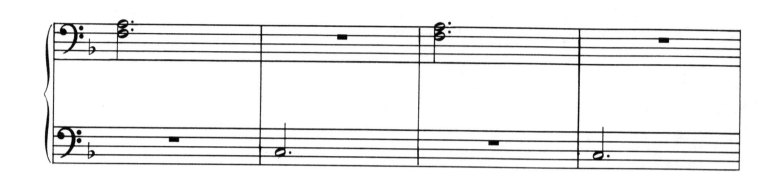

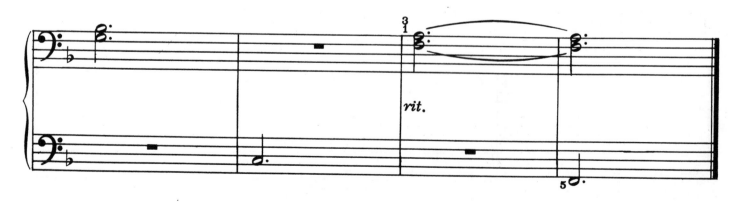

Primo

Both hands may be played one octave higher.

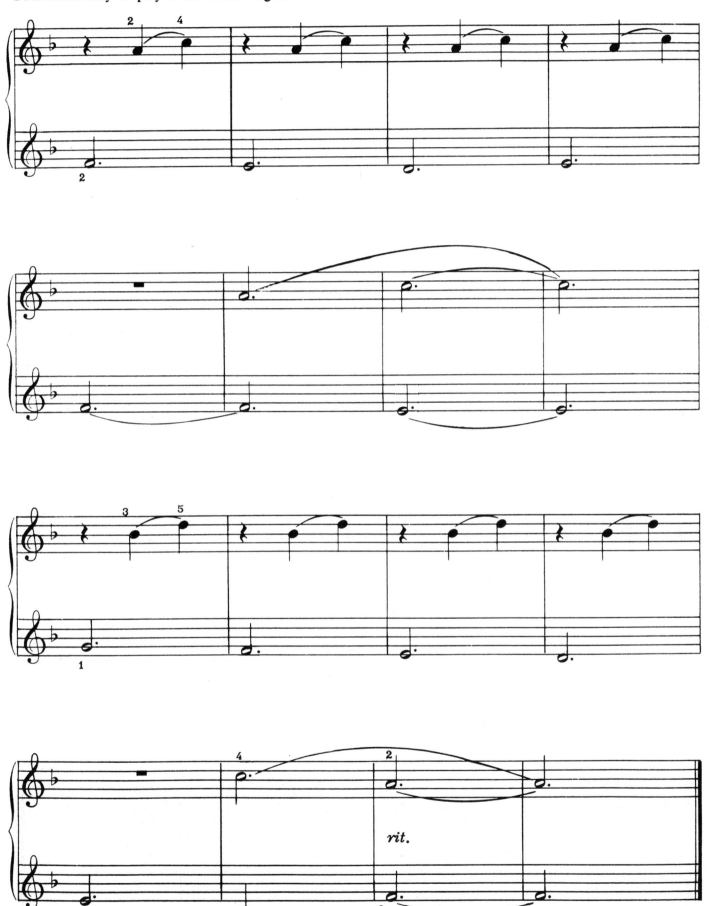

rit.

F.D.L.461

Prairie Grass

Secondo

Prairie Grass

Primo

Good Night, Ladies

Secondo

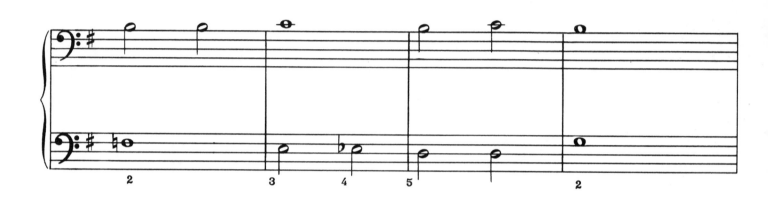

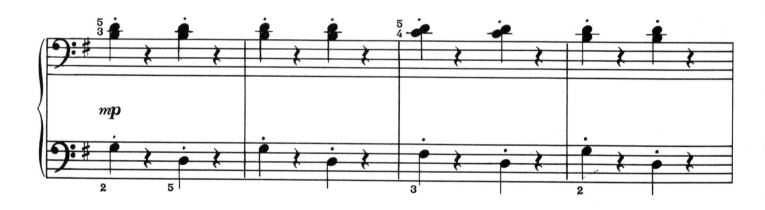

F.D.L.461

Good Night, Ladies

Primo

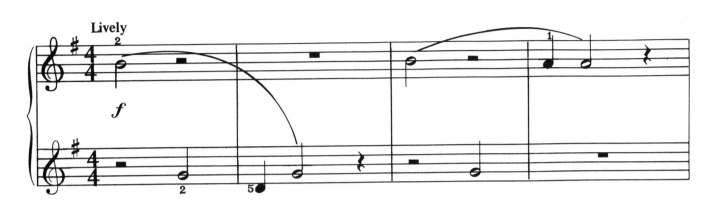

F.D.L.461

Secondo

Primo

F.D.L.461

I'm Sad

Secondo

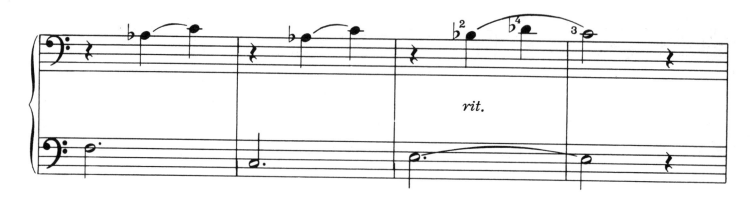

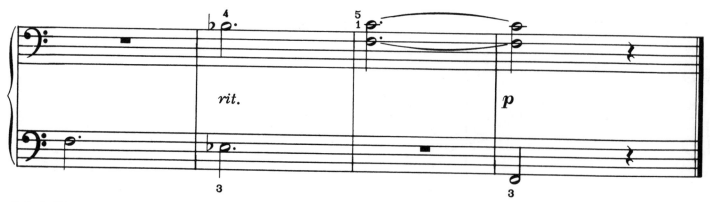

I'm Sad

Primo

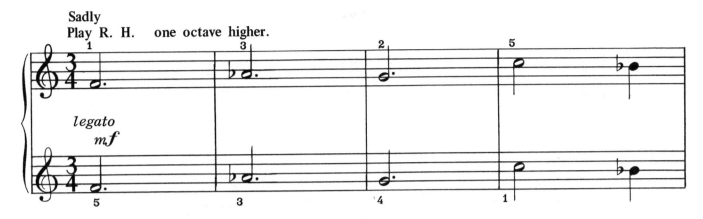

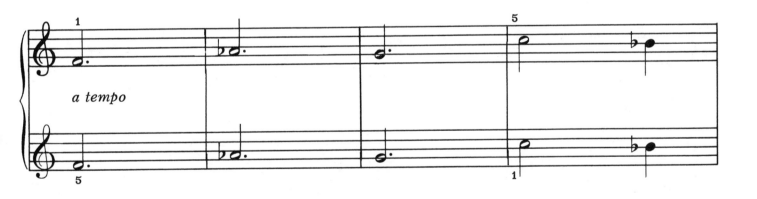

F.D.L.461

Witch Doctor

Secondo

Spooky

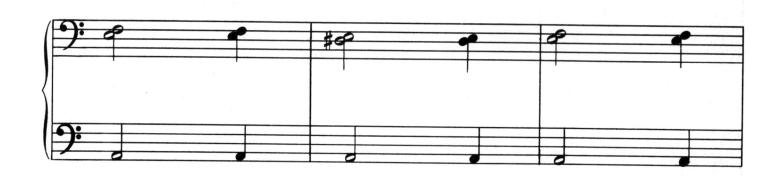

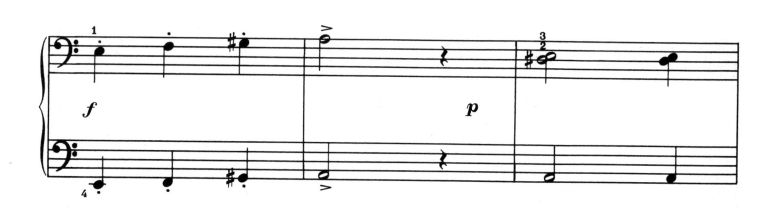

Witch Doctor

Primo

Secondo

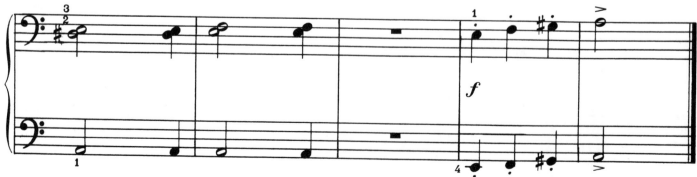

Both hands one octave lower.

Primo

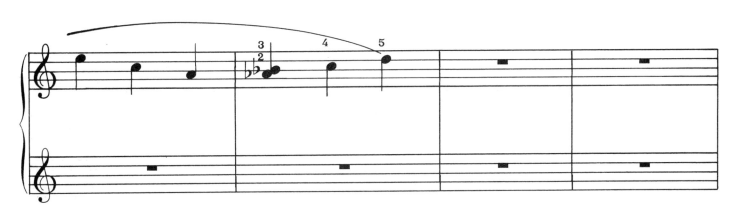

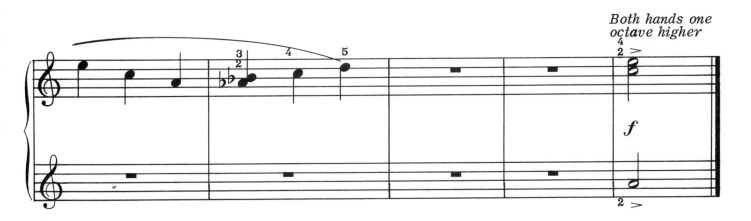

Riding A Cloud

Secondo

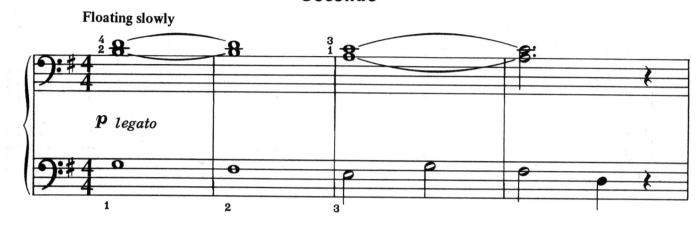

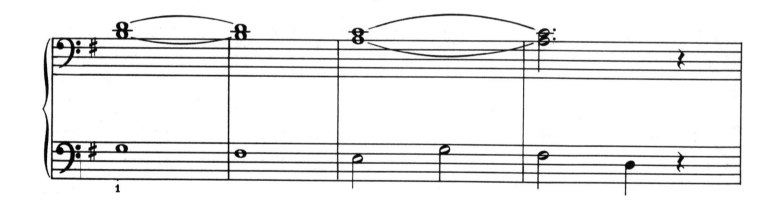

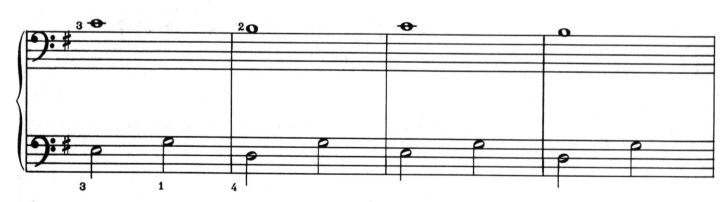

Riding A Cloud

Primo

Floating slowly

F.D.L.461

Secondo

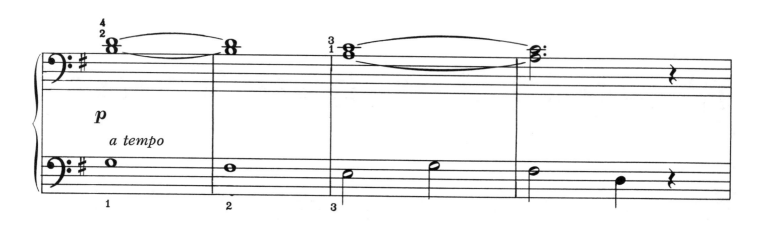

Primo

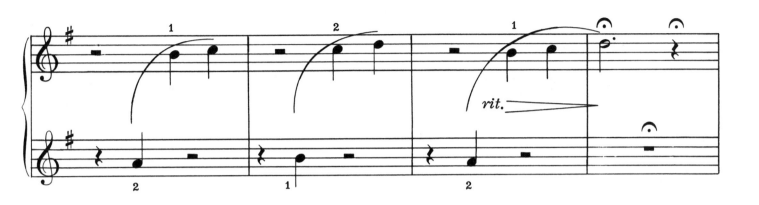

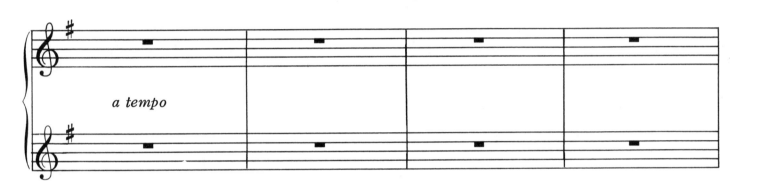

Both hands may be played one octave higher

F.D.L.461

Aura Lee

Secondo

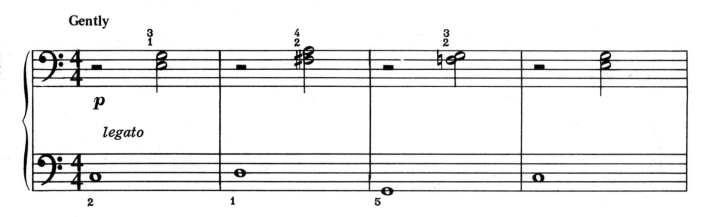

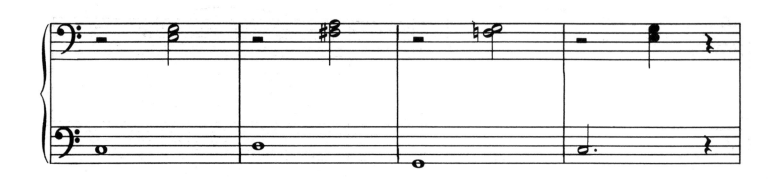

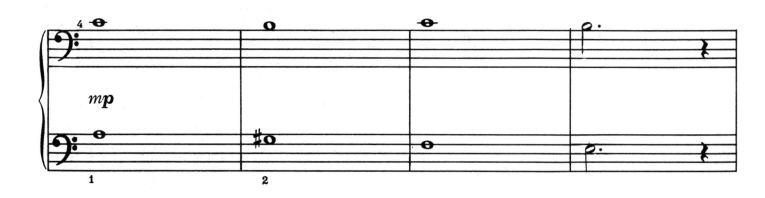

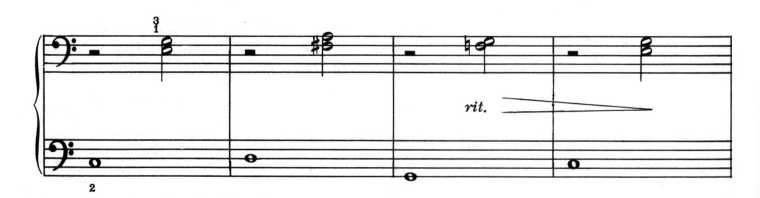

Aura Lee

Primo

Secondo

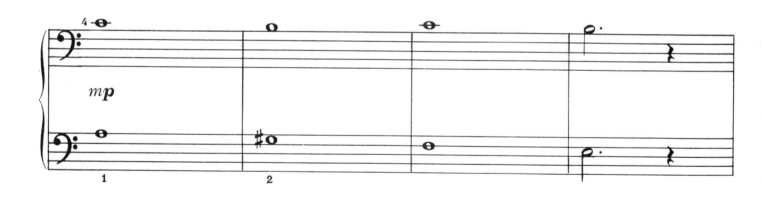

Primo

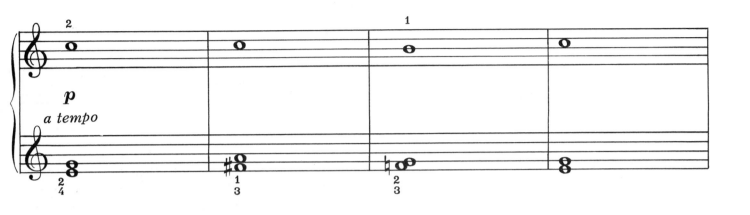

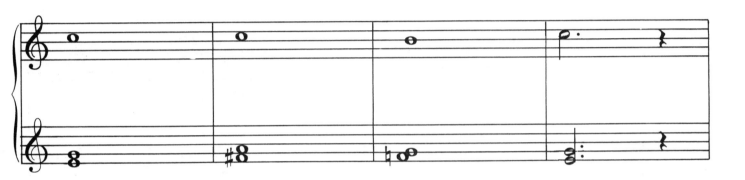

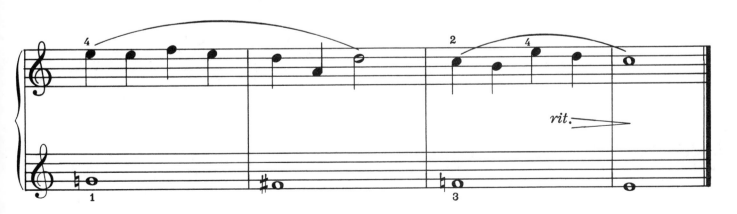

F.D.L.461

Turkey Trot

Secondo

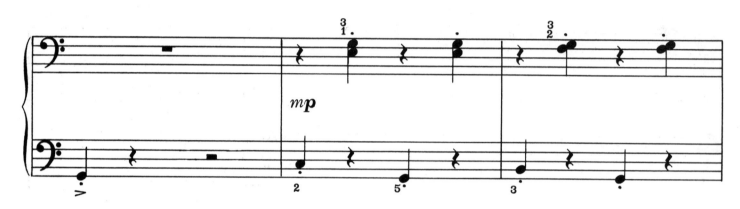

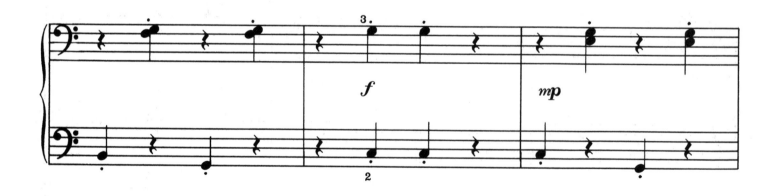

Turkey Trot

Primo

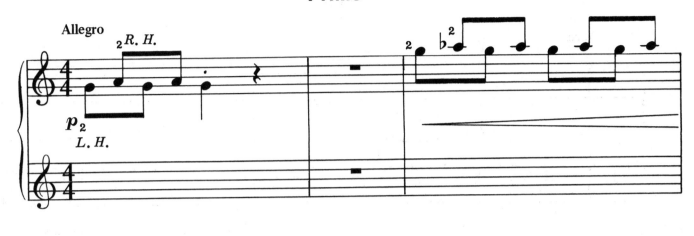

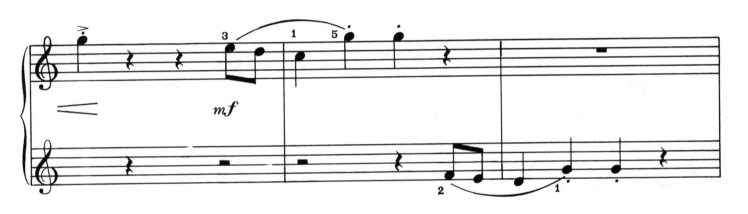

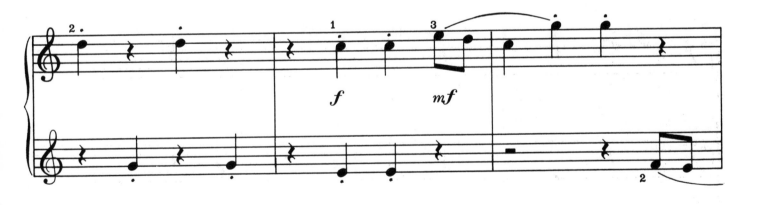

Secondo

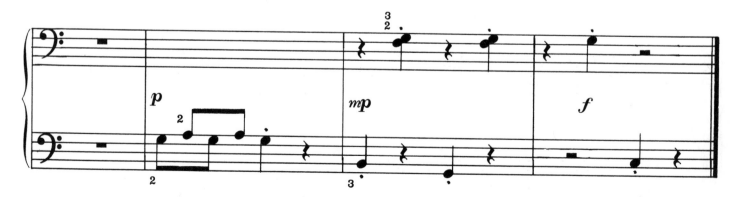

Primo

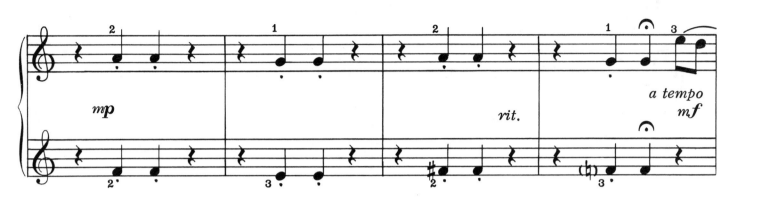

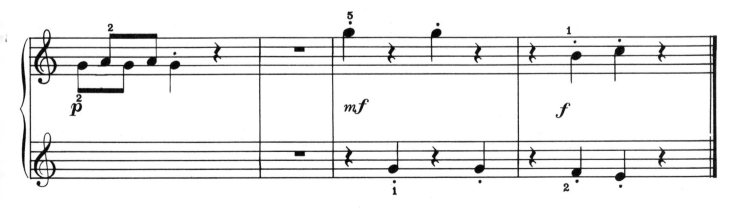

Russian Folk Music

Secondo

Russian Folk Music

Primo